Wayfinder

# Wayfinder

*new & selected poems*

Jan FitzGerald

STEELE ROBERTS
AOTEAROA

*To my husband Leonard Lambert,*
*and my children Harley, Angela and Jane.*

Acknowledgements: *Acumen (UK), Atlanta Review, Bridport Poetry Prize short list, Broadsheet, Cyclamens and Swords (Israel), The London Magazine, NZ Books, NZCEA English Level 1 syllabus, Poetry NZ, Takahe, Yellow Moon River (USA).*



Cover Design: Sarah Bolland
Production: Olivia Oravets

A catalogue record for this book is available from the National Library of New Zealand.

ISBN 978-0-947493-49-3

Steele Roberts Aotearoa
Box 9321 Wellington, Aotearoa New Zealand
info@steeleroberts.co.nz • www.steeleroberts.co.nz

## One poem

*I will move silently*
*through this world,*
*a mouse hole,*
*a gliding wing.*

*I will move only*
*to the unjangling*
*of your touch,*
*bird song at first rain,*
*the unshaven faces of ferns*
*pressing through the fence*

*and when the moon dibbles*
*across its feathered lake,*
*I will slip between soft waves,*
*leave behind*
*one poem worth the living.*

# Contents

## Letter to Tomé Torihama (1902–1992)

*Owner of Tomiya Restaurant, near Chiran Air Base,*
*who cared for kamikaze (tokkotai) pilots hours before*
*their last flight (and later, for American GIs.)*

How grateful
mothers must have been to you, Tomé-san,
your tears hidden by clouds of steam,
stirring your special rice
stained red by azuki beans,
for their sons' last meal.
Nothing too good for your boys,
your fireflies.

What were your thoughts
as you watched these young men in flight suits
drink miso soup, stroke the family cat?
How did a mother's heart cope with this,
knowing that out on the airfield
their flying coffins awaited?

It must have been painful
to hear Hiroshi play his bamboo flute
under your soft paper lanterns,
and Katsuo say,
I'm going to the next world at twenty,
but of the years I should have had,
I leave them to you.

How did it feel to watch them
walk off into the night towards the airfield,
their white scarves in the moonlight,
final letters to their mothers
in your hand?

In the morning
it was you, Tomé-san, at the runway,
waving a tattered Rising Sun, calling
*Goodbye Nobutaka, Chuji, Yukitoshi! Saburo!*
as they roared into a sky
that finished at Okinawa.

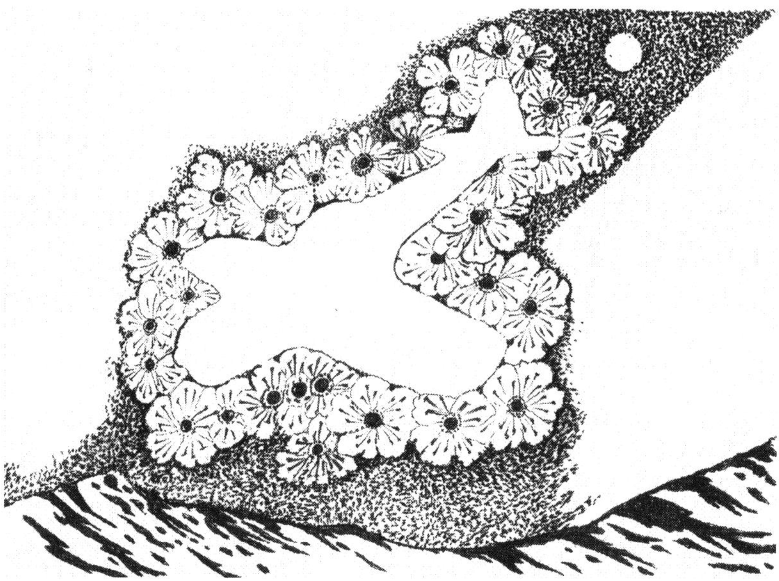

## Seahorse

Listen, little merman or mermaid,
those who say you're not a great swimmer,
evidently haven't met you underwater —
such superior buoyancy
belied by shyness.

I've watched you pass by
with the uprightness of charm school,
fanning the currents,
your blickering eye framed
in the fine bones of elegance.

How delicately you wrap your tail
around kelp, sway with the ocean, changing
your outfit to match the seaweed —
such self-effacement is barely credible.

Water dragon
Hippocampus
carrying yourself through reefs of coral
with calcified dignity

you're a shifting note
in one furious silence.

## Sky burial

And what if I had gone
really gone
and the soul departed
at the moment of death

would it be any different
if Tibetan friends
carried me on a yak
to the top of a mountain
and laid me out as alms
to another living creature?

Could it be any more barbaric,
the burial master's axe
splitting my ribcage,
blood spilling on the rocks
of a torn and lonely mountain,
than the secret embalmer
pouring my blood down a sluice,
injecting my veins
with formaldehyde
to preserve me.

Let the drums
and lama's incantations
summon the raptors,
their wings swirling
like flags on prayer wheels

let them feed
on a final act of charity.

Rather let me become part of a bird
than a worm,
my skeleton covered with the next snowfall,
the sky open in supplication

the yak that carried me set free.

## Wildebeest

Wildebeest line the clay banks
of the Mara river
like cave drawings against
ochre walls.

The air is hog-tied
by humidity.

The zebras among them are skittish,
on the point of stampede,
but there's nowhere to go.

Basking rocks are watching
for the weak, the orphaned.
Ears pricked,
the wildebeest wait.

A whip-crack of lightning
drives the pack forward,
nearer the water.

An old male
with the chest of an ox
and hindquarters of gazelle,
stands at the narrowest point of crossing,
stretches his noble neck
and sniffs the air.
Rain will swell the river.
He must jump.

He tosses his mane
and high-kicks the sky.
Crocodiles lunge upwards.
The herd launches itself,
eyes white and rolling.

The hesitant lose their grip
and slide into the river,
thrashing and screaming in
waves of red foam.

The muster moves south again
to the rhythm of rain,
the drum of Serengeti,
their Maasai mother.

*I am making clear streams*
*for you, a savannah bursting*
*with sweet buds and shoots*
*to wrap your tongues around.*

*My grasslands*
*will expose lion and hyena.*
*The hippo will bathe*
*in its muddy water hole.*

*Meerkats,*
*and baboons in lush trees,*
*will keep watch for you.*
*O my brave sons, my daughters!*

## War pigeons

1.

You were birds to be reckoned with,
hurtling through fiery branches
of tracer bullets
and above machine gun nests.

Released from wicker baskets
and tank turrets on the front line,
you flew through skies shaken
with falling planes and men.

From sinking bombers, flaming warships,
troops surrounded in dark forests,
you dashed with codes and co-ordinates,
in sights of sniper and enemy hawk.

2.

To *Cher Ami* who rescued a lost battalion
flying twenty one hours
with a bullet in the breast —
the Croix de Guerre.

To *2709*, from Passchendaele,
who flew with broken leg and shrapnel wounds,
delivered his message then died —
the PDSA Medal for Gallantry.

To *Winkie*, oil-coated and exhausted,
who covered over a hundred miles of ocean
when a bomber ditched in the North Sea —
the Dickin Medal.

And to the thousands of others who "Also Served,"
opening the door at last to your loft —
a soldier's dream of freedom
home to roost.

## Cows crossing

Cows slow the car to an indolent amble,
surround us with the pink mammary smell
of themselves.
Don't mind us, they say, and we won't mind you
as long as you fall in behind
learn how to cow-walk,
watch the marking of non-time
with our metronomic tails …
And what are you doing in that glass cage, anyway?
A bony head looms alongside
turning a neck a child would love to swing from,
a neck of teddy bear hair and old hay.
Her breath mists the window,
eyelashes come down
like slow camera shutters.

Never mind, never mind, it takes all sorts …
Her big, sassy hips sway past.
Move on, move on …
She is carrying a peach balloon to a party
that happened long ago.
Never mind, never mind …

## Netsuke

*(intricately carved Japanese ornament or toggle)*

This is the ritual of handling.
My fingers tiptoe over
a samurai kneeling.

Each rivulet in his robe
draws me in, every strand
of his topknot.

The carver's
energy is released
and enshrined.

Hand on sword,
the samurai bows.

To the Emperor.
To the enemy.

Through fluid lines
this object of exactitude
deigns to enter

the internal maps
of consciousness

where dignity and violence engage
in rosewood and ivory.

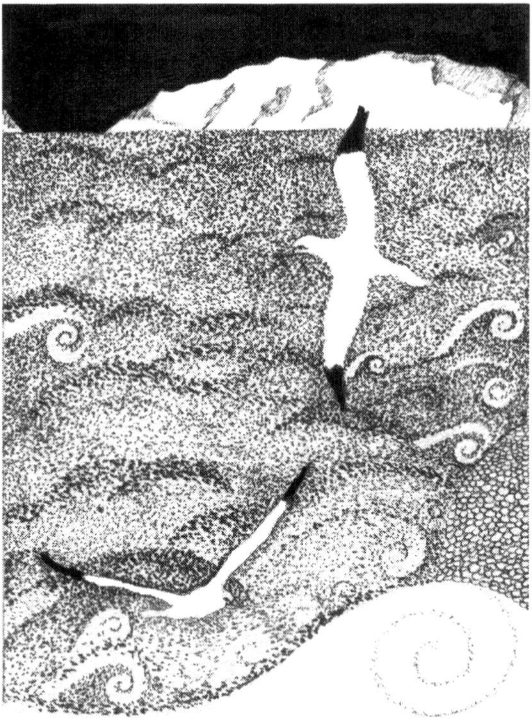

## Gannets

Heads brushed with sea pollen,
they ride the thermals up to height,
tease out the sky
hover
take aim

d i v e.

A stratospheric entry
plume of spray!
shake the head
slip the fish
flap the wings twice …

Eyes alive with bright harbours
they hunt the waves,
beaks sharpened on surprise
glide up
bank east
barrel-roll …

d i v e.

## Sea captain

Time sinks into the grass
and dredges up the smell of the ocean.
Here, the man from Hull,
apprentice of the North Sea,
spread his net across the lawn,
over the trees,
a trellis for fish to climb.

All day
he gathered tangle up to his lap,
fingers full of knots & nimble,
a man goading tides
through his own back yard,
canary & English wife at porthole

all day,
roughness tenderly threaded,
coaxing out the woman's name
of each trawler
caught with a full catch in a storm …

Now in a pensioner flat,
galleons drowning
on the mantel,
compass & barometer
on the wall,
an old woman listens
to a crackling ship's radio

waiting for Jack to come home.

## When I die

When I die make me a nest,
a hay-bed
in a seaward tree —

let my bones lie
a bundle of white branches
dividing the wind's secrets,

north from north-east.

Let me hear
the name of each wave
returning

understand
the Morse tapping
of birds in their shells

see the light
of answering cries
over water.

Let my bones lie
hearing the details
of moonlight

the amplified vastness
of love
& all things

surprising.

## Cricket girl

Because its song was lucky
and told when spring was come,
her father let her keep the cricket indoors,
so he'd know when it was time for planting.

Because the cricket's song was earthy and sweet,
like dirt on new potatoes,
she'd press her lips to the cage at night
and whisper secrets to it.

"This cricket is a *dichong*," she'd say,
to anyone who'd listen,
"caught near my village,
not by peasants in the fields
for ugly sport of cricket fighting."
She twirled the brass cage
so light flickered like dragonflies
stitched in gold on her dress.

Later, with a handful of coins
from selling goat cheese at the market,
she rescued many crickets
destined to be fighters.

Her father, driven crazy by the trilling, said.
"You are lucky it is unlucky
to release them.
If you want to have so many crickets
you must sleep with the goats."

So she did.

## Chrysalis

In the morning it hangs
like a tiny jade house
with spots of gold for adornment,
roof trussed with shining thread.

Yet the miracle is not
a winged sylph
emerging from a liquid,
but a butterfly inside a caterpillar,
four generations in a year
laid down on imaginal discs.

Carrying inside you
wings legs antennae proboscis
you rake back and forth
on potted swan plant in the kitchen,
while a distant cousin makes
a climate deal in Canada
for warmer weather in Mexico.

Laying down your silk button,
you delve inside yourself
for the cremaster,
the wand that attaches you
to another world,
then you split, the curtains part
on kabuki theatre.
A shapeshifter appears.
He writhes and contorts
to shed his dark kimono

and, in the morning, look!
A tiny house of jade.

## A mother's magic

I never could imagine
how mother knew such magic,
stirring her secret potions —
mint leaves floating
in a jug of vinegar and brown sugar,
sliced peaches kayaking
in a bubbling whirlpool.
Silverbeet flowed over the bench
like a wave of kelp.
She created worlds.

From under the kitchen table,
where history's told
in the silver tones of spiders,
I listened to her spells,
the poetry, the utterance,
occasional disaster
for which mice and I were grateful.

Until peekaboo-where-are-you!
A giant face peering under,
breath like a warm scone,
eyes all spritz & binkle.
I yanked the cloth
and the sky collapsed.
All upside-down and milk crying.

## Ticket 250654 RMS *Titanic*

*A tribute to band leader Wallace Hartley (1878–1912)*

As a line of First Class passengers
left the lounge in canvas life vests,
and like a migration of white crabs
shuffled towards the sea,
you played to them.

On an April night like no other,
you gathered your men on the boat deck
and above shouts of "Women and children first!"
and screams of disbelief,
you played the violin
your Maria had given you,
until the last lifeboat pulled away.

Then waist-deep in icy waters,
under the illuminated dome
of the Grand Staircase
and tilt of groaning funnels,
you strapped the violin to yourself,
bade your colleagues farewell
and bowed to the drums of the North Atlantic.

## The cormorants

*(NZ shag)*

Judges in black gowns,
a triumvirate of shags
presides over the bay.
Every day
on the same dead branch
they sit in sworn silence,
dumb as rocks,
waiting on the tide
to present itself.

The sentence will be severe.

In a splash
the judges are gone
and serpents with feathers
whip through an underworld
of slip-gullet herring
and groaning seaweed.
Dark streaks
of raid and plunder,
lean with the hunt
and oil preened, they loop
and turn, and finally
break into air,
with a toss of beak —
summary justice!

The tide goes out.
The judges return to the bench,
lunch recess over.

## Winter

Rain mollifies,
the wind goes to ground,
and we sit listening
like creatures in a vast acreage
to the tiniest *plip* of water,
or the click of carbon atoms locking
into place in the earth
far below

and somewhere
after two hundred million years,
a piece of carbon
under pressure unimaginable,
extrudes upwards
and cools as diamond

in a day devoid of hurry,
where dandelions carry on
their quiet alchemy,
and the only thing certain
is winter.

## Miss Molloye

A stranger has moved in upstairs.
He sits with a face as blank as alabaster
and scrapes the labels off words.

She feels a grief behind the eyelids.
Did I once have a lover?
For a moment she knows.

She knows that she knows …
then it goes again.

Why is he emptying the cupboards?
Such a rummage of silverfish!
He's stolen the notes from the music sheet!

What delicate fingers I have.
Did I ever play the piano?

She looks out on flowers
someone planted long ago.

The man opens a window.
Words flutter down and beyond.
She hears a familiar voice
but can't catch the tune.

Why has he changed the lock,
hidden all the photographs?

The keys swing out of reach
of the keyhole.

Why must that woman in the mirror
always talk when I'm talking?

## Cycling

Unravelled from the world,
riding high,
pushing west,
the sound
of air rushing,
spokes singing.
Dotterels
sprint ahead,
drawing us into their decoy,
this way, this way,
away from the nest,
away from the town.
We are dots diminishing.
Storming an incline,
we are hooked to the hills
flaring ahead,
the cloud-banked horizon
arguing humidity.
Swallows shoot by
as the wind sucks
at teats of landscape.
We lean on the sky
this way
and that
the sound
of air rushing.

## Aubade

Your voice from the sheets,
a lifeline to the long teardrop
that plumbs my underworld.

All night possums hung
from consumptive breaths,
owls shrunk the windows.
The hill turned inward
forgetting what summer was.

Now your words unstitch
the moon's mouth, your kiss
becalms the barking stars,
dumbs the wind.

## Family tree

Into the light of night they come,
these familiar shadows,
with faces known — yet not.

A definite nose,
a smile,
the way a lock falls … Patrick Murphy,

in the year of the Potato Famine,
with a regiment
of Irish Fencibles. Jonah Russ,

from rural Somerset, landing
in New Zealand without a shilling
to bless him. John Davies,

a good-looking Welshman,
without any history. Lucy Murcott,

spinster with two children
and no father registered,
a place in Nelson named after her. Esau Russ,

twin and stablehand,
shot dead
over the naming of a foal. Job's wife,

Elizabeth, mother of ten,
survivor of a great sea journey,
dying from a slip on the verandah. A baby

stillborn on Christmas Day,
buried under an apple tree. John Wright,

sentenced to death in England
for stealing four sheep
to feed a large family. Children

lost to chicken pox and typhus,
buried at sea.

Carpenters, bricklayers, farmers,
women in bonnets and gloves.
Grandmothers — fathers — and greats,

such familiar shadows,
gently turning over my clothes,
wondering what to make of my life.

# Highland cattle-beast

I don't see him at first
underneath the canopy of vines,
shaggy and still
as a grandmother's fur coat
at the back of a wardrobe.

One hoof moves, then another,
as he edges toward me.
The great horns dip and tilt,
lifting foliage away,
gentle as a hunter's hand.
Twigs bury themselves
in the mud of No Noise.

Druid leaves have lent
their russet to him, his backbone
is the craggy ridge of a hill.
What do you say to a behemoth
standing before you?

An eye kind as a wishing well
considers me.
Am I the being from the tall macrocarpa trees?
I daren't touch him.
His breath is mossy and shy
as the dust of an archaeological find.

## Ruaumoko

*(God of earthquakes)*

I have hung
the tiniest of temple bells
outside my studio

to change the sound
of your footsteps.

From now on
you will announce yourself
at the door

in a way I can imagine
a visit

from the Dalai Lama.

## The doll

There are no rheumy knuckles
on my porcelain fingers.
I have the cheeks of certain cherubim.
Even my armpits are smug.

I hold the penny-farthing handlebars.
Its high wheel diminishes my face
and my legs become eye-height.
Pollards bollards knickerbockers
and bockety bumps.

My long ribbed stockings
so delicate in riding boots …
the smell of leather protects me.
*Ringabel ringabel*
Out of my way top hats, waistcoats
fob watches, cravats!

"Annabel …" the doctor called.
The nurse rearranged the flowers
just before she left.

I'm tall as a horse, a hawthorn bush,
my head rushing along the hedgerows,
the checkerboard fields.
The barn cries out Hello!
I'm a Snug in a tartan riding cape,
a flapping of wings.
My face disappears, a crochet hook
is pulling in all the loose ends.
A nose wedded to a lace handkerchief,
brass buttons, kiss-prints left by elves.
No one to catch me, smack me,
pull me out from under the bed.

Annabel … I can see you …
The nurse was kind but she left.

*Ringabel Annabel*
chant the birds from broken nests.
A crocheted heart without a birthmark,
a glass eye without a tear,
I spin through poles of autumn
like a holocaust of leaves.

*Ringabel Annabel,*
who would have guessed.

## The joy gatherers

1.

He loved frost for its honesty
and grapefruit with no agenda
but the gift of marmalade.

Some days he would sit in the orchard,
cigarette between yellow fingers,
and watch morning in buddha robes
come swinging its censers
of sunlight.

"Two shillings in the pound,"
the locals said, but the spinster who hired him
and the little girl who watched him
knew better.

His hands held a codlin moth's
knowledge of apple trees,
and under the béret that roamed his head
like a cat pawing its bed before sleep,
lay secrets that could make branches
ignite with spring.

Afternoons he lay on a burlap sack
on the mound of cuttings
and stared up at the canopy of blossom
where God lived.

2.

On the other side of town,
a man shambled along the foreshore,
sack slung over back,
eyes fixed on the low tide mark,
the wobbling gramophone needle
of a song he could not resist.

The locals called him Spring-Heeled Jack.
Respected naturalist came later.

He died in his hut, alone,
on the Papahenga salt marsh,
Michael Hodgkins and his dog,
paintings by his famous aunt
blocking holes in the wall.

## Holding a tuatara

Still as her two million years,
she lies in my hand.
One eye rolls back
to study me.

Her body, stickled
and rock-barked,
is in no rush
to go anywhere.

Her cold underbelly
settles into my palm.

I hold a skin bag of pebbles!
Claws rest on my fingers
like bracken.

She opens her mouth.
It's not a voice you hear
but a sound you know —
your mother calling you
in a dream,
or a larrup of stones
falling into a cave.

I am not fooled by the tail
draped over my arm.

Any second now
she could flash that fossil head
and crack my wrist bone.

## Bees

My mother's old honey pot,
a pollen mosque,
sits on the kitchen table,
while the bees of childhood
thrum midday prayers
inside this citadel of nectar.

Bees, amber and drizzled
with the ooze
of over-ripe apples,
treading the leaves
in my father's wheelbarrow,
juicing the warmth
of autumn.

1967
a boyfriend
in spacesuit and gloves,
holding up a seething honeycomb
as mini soldiers crawl,
bayonets fixed,
with rucksacks of venom
over my netting visor.

Years later
my children fleeing
along a country road,
stumbling
and panting and yelling,
chased by a groaning cloud,
with a voice as thick as treacle.

## Mr Rogers

Even the school bully called you Dad
at least once by mistake.
From the day we reached the Standards,
we all wanted to be in your class.
It wasn't just the bomber jacket
and moustache that set you apart,
but the fact you were on playground duty
every day of the week.

What a transformation
when the boys kicked the ball your way —
from a man cupping a fag against the wind
to a lanky forward dodging up the field,
boys flailing and falling into laughing bundles
of missed tackles.

One day in the sweet, grass smell of summer
that blew down from the haybaling hills,
you were gone.
The new teacher didn't help the boys
with their model Spitfires,
or look up at the sky
when the midday siren wailed.

Nobody knew much about you.
My father said that wasn't such a bad thing.
"The man's ex-RAF — and that's good enough for me."
Our neighbour said, "The minute the 3 o'clock bell rang,
he used to pack the kiddies' books in his satchel
and head straight up to the local."
Dad said, How did she know?

I imagined you sitting in the corner,
our books all marked and stacked,
signing copies of *Biggles*.

Rumour had it you went south to dry out.
You never did come back.
But the day a Vulcan jet
swooped so low over the playground
the headmaster hit the ground,
Jimmy Sharplin swore he saw you
waving from the cockpit.

## Yesterway

Some things you pick up
because you can't leave them —
a coin on the pavement,
a small copper etching of a house
orphaned in an op shop.

Later when you clean it,
look closer, something trembles
the soil by the gate,
daffodil shoots unfurling
towards the tip of darkness.

A postman blows his whistle
and a figure smaller
than you would ever remember
opens the door,
trundles down the path.

Taking scissors from her apron,
she snips a daffodil, welcomes you in
down the dark hallway
through the bright kitchen —
blackberry jam on the stove,
scones on the windowsill.

You follow her
out the back door,
out to the meadow,
under trees billowing
like clouds of rosellas

and she shows you
how to attend
in the pause before green,
in the space between raindrops,
how to listen with your feet

and hear the world stop.

## Mike

The photo in the lounge told the story.
A handsome man sitting on a hay bale in a barn
flanked by his wife, four children
and six border collies
their ruffs ribboned with medals.

Other dogs he had buried under the willows
each with its own headstone.
He would greet them
as he drove by on the tractor
*Morning Georgie! Champ! Flicker!*
And somewhere
from the fresh-mown hay
smell of sun on the river stones
they'd answer.

And so it was each morning
that we held him up in the hoist
and removed his pyjamas to wash him
face hands armpits chest belly privates
eased on his rugby shorts
settled him in the wheelchair
put on his fleecy checked shirt
and the hat crowned with winning dog badges
laced up his boots
fed him his porridge and cup of tea …
wheeled him into the hospital lounge
by his photo

left him calling out
*Hunter! Flash! Shadow! Mac! Bailey! Jess!*

## In memory of Budgie B. Bird

Where your cage hung there is a space
of transparent lines and abandoned angles.
A square of time has emptied its pockets.

The turban of song
you wound around us
has unravelled
and trails out over the garden,
over hopping-sad bugs and glum flowers,
through bald gum trees with their black rook cries
and barren nests.

A crowd of inconsolable clouds gathers.
The impossible sky has a hole in it,
the shape of a small, blue bird that passed through it
on her journey to a well-worn perch
in the place of Nothing Doing,
Everything Sung.

## Fire!

Terrified by what we might see,
we ran from our beds to the edge of the bank,
scanning the black estuary.
Here in the daytime, daffodils,
leggy ballerinas,
had shivered in the wind —
how had we travelled so fast
from innocent to ominous,
deafened by this crackling?

Was it a fire without flames
creeping through the toetoe?
A fire that fed on darkness?
The night was tight-lipped,
the moon, Methuselah-hag, shuffled
across the mudflats on her sticks
of pohutukawa.

Crabs!
It was crabs up from their caverns,
clack-clacking their claws,
snipping the air with bony scissors.
Crabs,
in their white evening jackets,
courting the world
with such loud kisses!

## Afterwards

*for LL*

…and afterwards, the slowing of time.
A gliding of wings above the bed.
The silence

when a tree receives the song

of its tenant,

night hears a fish crawl out of a pond.
When we return from Molentol, carrying

the sheen of the river.

Your eyes full of music … And the world, apparently,

somewhere

outside.

## Old orchard

Heaven
has pitched its tent here,
opened its awning
to four tastes of summer.

The pear tree leans
on guy ropes of sky.

In the grove
cool with bamboo,
fantails unpin a topknot of straw,
trail its tresses
through a comb of branches.

In the neighbouring field of corn,
each cob
in readiness with its silken cord.

## Cricket riff

In the cleared plot next door
a cricket nails it
with a song,
quite the dude
in night's tuxedo.

No longer
the derelict house
and druggies, but a sweet solo
of freedom, syrupy
as a saxophone

jamming on —
his two sleek batons
conducting an orchestra of one

something smooth and black
and soulful —
jamming all night

up from the underground
to all that is new and good
a herald
of something higher and better
like the voice of a new moon

in the bitter shoots of oxalis
and coolness of grass —
jamming all night

bring it on maestro
bring it on

## Moana-nui-a-Kiwa

Lying outside the door of the hut
at night, she listens
to the mother-beat of the ocean,
the slow hisssh of tumbling shells
as the water recedes.

*I was born with surf in my bones.*

Times like these
spellbound by sound,
the waves of her mother's womb,
she is tethered to a deep simplicity.
Times like these
friends and school wash away.

Her grandmother said,
pointing to her chiseled tattoo
on lips and chin,
"This means all rivers lead to the ocean."
It was blue like squid ink.

Lying outside in the cool grass,
looking up at stars of the Milky Way
like mother-of-pearl pieces,
she listens
in the silence before the wave cracks,
to the silver voices of fish

sermons of the sea.

## In praise of bees

The bees are at it again —
a flash-mob orchestra,
Wild Honey Band —
swaying blossoms
in the orchard
on a stopover
between Clover and Thistle.

Can any conductor's baton
be so precious
as a stamen
that brings forth such music,
wings fanning deep notes
of amber and cello?

Can any artist
match the genius
of a bricolage
built with wax and nectar?

The bees are back
in the orchestra pit
with tubular bells
and trumpets, gold tuxedos
humming in sunlight

making honey
that sings in the mouth.

## Frogs

You watched us
as we ran home from school
holding down our skirts —

slobber monsters
with swampmoon eyes
that rose from puddles
and winked.

You knew all our shortcuts,
every alley, every path,
as you surfed down teeming gutters
and clambered out of drains.

We ran from your flypaper tongues,
suckered fingers that stretched and stuck.
In the school baths, you goobed our hair
with jellied rafts of spawn.

Now we live in a world without
your dancing on the road
holding silver strings of rain,
your broken-cello arguments.

You've disappeared and we're to blame.
I miss you,
you goitred little blowhards.

## Whale

Whale, if you were a hat
you'd be a homburg.
If you were an actor,
you'd be Gérard Depardieu.

If you were a ship
you'd be a sunken galleon,
blowing beluga bubbles
five hundred years old.

If you were furniture,
you'd be a chest freezer
with a bellyful of mayhem.
If a house, an old villa,
with a ribcage of rafters.

But what you are is Whale,
Arrluk and Cetus,
heart and heartbeat of Ocean.

## Wayfinder

*Homage to the early Polynesian navigator*

This waka I guide with chant and song
for this is the whakapapa of past voyages,
the voice of my ancestors
who went fishing for islands.

We leave at dusk, our eyes fixed
on landmarks behind us.
By looking backwards,
I chart the way forward.

I observe the stars in Tane's Basket.
Each one known by name since childhood.
Each one cloaked in a different brightness.

I recall the clouds that name an island,
reflections that warn of reefs or shallows.
Some clouds mirror the island beneath.

Each wind brings its own song
to the rigging, hangs up a cloak feathered
with many scents.

Migrating birds show me the seasons.
I study curlew, plover, long-tailed cuckoo.
The albatross studies me …
At dusk birds fly in straight lines
to their island.

If I sleep and stray off course,
I am woken by drumming under the hull.
Each current has its own rhythm.
I adjust to the rope that trails
the original path.

I know the waves
that mark the approach to each harbour,
like the way hair flows on the back of a dog.
As each one breaks against the bow,
it tells of distance or nearness.

When Hoaka, the crescent moon, rises
she scares the fish away, being the first moon
bright enough to cast a shadow.
When Muku is in the sky,
it is a night of good fishing.

I give the first of my catch back to Tangaroa,
not knowing if the shadow below
is hammerhead or taniwha,
not knowing if I anger or appease him

if tonight is the night I will catch an island.

**Jan FitzGerald**

Any reader of the literary journals of the late 1960s and '70s would have noted the name Jan Coad. Hone Tuwhare certainly did, and James K. Baxter, from both of whom Jan received admiration and friendship.

In 2005 writing under her married name, FitzGerald, Jan launched her long-gestated collection, *Flying Against the Arrow* (Wolfdale Press). This was followed by *On a Day Like This* (Steele Roberts Aotearoa, 2010).

All the while, the poet was quietly maturing as an artist, and in this collection, for the first time, the two talents perform a happy tango.